Acknowledgments

Alice Hoffman. From "It's a Wonderful House" by Alice Hoffman, first printed in *Architectural Digest*, December 1993. All rights reserved.

Joyce Carol Oates. From "Coming Home" by Joyce Carol Oates. Copyright © 1995 by The Ontario Review, Inc. Reprinted by permission of John Hawkins & Associates, Inc.

This book has been bound using hand-craft methods, and is Smyth-sewn to ensure durability.

The cover and interior were illustrated by Barbara Strawser.

The dust jacket and interior were designed by Corinda J. Cook.

The text was edited by Tara Ann McFadden.

The text was set in Cochin.

HOME

A Little Book of Comfort

RUNNING PRESS
PHILADELPHIA · LONDON

Library of Congress Cataloging-in-Publication Number 96–67147
ISBN 1–56138–751–7

This book may be ordered by mail from the publisher.
Please include $1.00 for postage and handling.
But try your bookstore first!

Running Press Book Publishers
125 South Twenty-second Street
Philadelphia, Pennsylvania 19103–4399

Contents

 # *Introduction*

Blue shutters, white paint, and a picket fence. Two bedrooms with a spacious living room and wood-burning fireplace. A studio apartment with a great view. Your home. It's where you spend the most time with the people you love most.

When we dream about our life or remember where we've been, our home is the place foremost in our minds. It is the center stage of our lives. Home is where you share laughter, dreams, accomplishments, and love with friends and family.

A home says a lot about the people who live in it. Whether you have tie-dyed curtains and a mattress on the floor, or a Chippendale sofa and matching armoire,

7

there is a special warmth and intimacy found in every home. Homes are made—not from bricks and mortar but from scratches on the table, dents in the walls, and fingerprints on the wallpaper. Its music is the ringing of phones, the shouting of the children, and soft laughter on a summer's night.

Homes are built or restored, cared

for and loved with a special reverence.

They're safe places where people can

grow, learn, and love. Within these

pages are fond memories and universal

dreams that began, like life, in the home.

Housewarming

That people could come into the world in a place they could not at first even name and had never known before; and that out of a nameless and unknown place they could grow and move around in it until its name they knew and called with love . . . HOME, and put roots there and love others there; so that whenever they left this place they would sing homesick songs about it and write poems of yearning for it . . . .

William Goyen (1915–1983)
American writer

'Mid pleasures and palaces though we
   may roam,
Be it ever so humble, there's no place
   like home.

J. H. Payne (1842–1916)
English poet and translator

Home, in one form or another, is the great object of life.

Josiah Gilbert Holland (1819–1881)
American editor and writer

. . . I am absolutely sure I knew it
even then. I knew it the way . . .
when you see a particular house on a
particular landscape you think: Yes,
that is for me, I am going to live there.

Anita Shreve (b. 1947)
American writer

To most men their early home is no more than a memory of their early years. The image is never marred. There's no disappointment in memory, and one's exaggerations are always on the good side.

George Eliot [Mary Ann Evans]
(1819–1880)
English writer

I loved the house the way you would any new house, because it is populated by your future. the family of children who will fill it with noise and chaos and satisfying busy pleasures.

Jane Smiley (b. 1949)
American writer

I took my time exploring. I savored the first few minutes in a new home . . . I stepped stealthily over the bare floors, peeking around corners and into alluring doors, which generally turned out to be the broom closet. But there was a thrilling sense in that, like a new lover, the place held attributes I had yet to discover. . . .

Barbara Kingslover (b. 1955)
American writer

The most beautiful place on earth,
our childhood home.

Peggy Jones
20th-century American writer

from "Coming Home"

Is it possible to have two or even three homes, simultaneously? An adolescent's incandescent passion for each, equally?

From Syracuse University I went, in the fall of 1960, to the University of Wisconsin at Madison. Where, within an absurdly romantic compressed period of time, I fell in love. (He was an "older" man—a Ph.D. student in English literature. I was a beginning M.A. student.) We met on October 23, were engaged on November 23, and were married on January 23, 1961, amid the subfreezing winds for which UW-Madison is renowned. Home was suddenly an elegantly spacious five-room furnished apartment on the second floor of a private house on University Avenue, about a mile from campus. My first home as a married woman . . . glimmers in my memory as a place of transcendental happiness; though I must have felt some measure of scholarly anxiety, rising very early, at dawn, leaving my sleeping husband to sit in an oversized chair by a window in the living room, there to study, study, study—Old English vocabulary and grammar, Middle English (Chaucer's Canterbury Tales), and the long-forgotten drama of the pre-Shakespearean stage, and so on, and on. On windy days, we walked homeward from the campus in a trance of longing. And though I lived in Madison for only eight brief months, somehow it came to be, by a process of assimilation, that this admirable university town became home as well; home that was, and still is, the specific atmosphere of college—the haven of great libraries, bookstores, university buildings of some architectural distinction; trees, pathways, sloping green lawns.

I live now in a sprawling one-story house with numerous glass walls and sky-lights, about four miles south of Princeton. My husband and I have lived here since 1978, having bought this house, now to us the quintessence of home, in a single Sunday afternoon of house-hunting. Everyone says

that the house seems made for us, or us
for it; yet of course it was an accident that
it was waiting for us, an emblem now of our
Princeton lives.

. . . That place where, when we go there,
the door is already open, we are being greeted;
where, when I return to my study, to my desk,
I will discover a single rose, or a small
flowering plant, waiting for me.

Joyce Carol Oates (b. 1938)
American writer

I suppose I was eight or nine before I discovered the pleasures of the fig tree, and although I have lived in many houses since then, including a few I made for myself, I still think of it as my first and most beloved home.

Lillian Hellman (1905–1984)
America playwright

The house we were born in is more than an emobodiment of home, it is also an embodiment of dreams. Each one of its nooks and corners was a resting-place for daydreaming.

Gaston Bachelard (1884–1962)
French philosopher and writer

from "My Early Home"

The old house stooped just like a cave,
*   Thatched o'er with mosses green;*
Winter around the walls would rave,
*   But all was calm within;*
The trees are here all green agen,
*   Here bees the flowers still kiss,*
But flowers and trees seemed sweeter then:
*   My early home was this.*

John Clare (1793–1864)
English poet

What is the perfect way to happiness?
To stay at home.

Bhartṛhari (c. 570–651)
Indian philosopher and poet

It never occurred to me until I had this house to take a vacation and stay home.

Bill Robiason
20th-century American decorator

Rooms of Our Own

Nothing can replace the shock of
pleasure given by a small mountain of
fresh basil in the summer kitchen. . . .

Eleanor Perényi (b. 1918)
American writer

Think this over carefully: the most charming hours of our life are all connected—by a more or less tangible hyphen—with a memory of the table.

Pierre-Charles Monselet (1825–1888)
French writer and gastronome

. . . the kitchen, the house's warm heart.

Anne Rivers Siddons (b. 1936)
American writer

When you have a party at home, no matter how much room you have, the guests will automatically manage to work their way into the kitchen. . . . Warmth and food and life.

Mary Higgins Clark (b. 1929)
American writer

. . . people's living space and the personal possessions with which they surrounded themselves were inevitably fascinating . . . an affirmation of identity, intriguing both in themselves and as a betrayal of character, interests, obsessions.

P. D. James (b. 1920)
English writer

Rooms are like people. It takes time to get to know them. And even then, the interesting ones keep revealing themselves more and more.

Jane Stanton Hitchcock (b. 1953)
American writer and playwright

My house is a metaphor for my life:
The better it looks on the surface,
the more chaos I'm hiding in the drawers
and closets.

Linda Henley (b. 1951)
American writer

I had no money to buy art, so I would buy old picture frames and put them on white walls, just framing space, which I thought was beautiful.

Barbra Streisand (b. 1942)
American singer, songwriter,
actress, and director

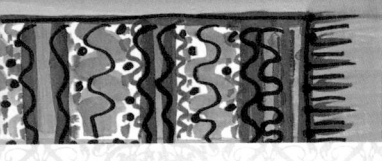

People create their habitation in their own image.

Pearl S. Buck (1892–1963)
American writer

To build a house is one thing, but to make it a home is quite another. . . .

Louis L'Amour (1908–1988)
American writer

Have nothing in your house that you do not know to be useful, or believe to be beautiful.

William Morris (1834–1896)
English poet

A house that does not have one worn, comfy chair in it is soulless.

May Sarton (1912–1995)
American writer

Any piece of furniture, I don't care how beautiful it is, has got to be lived with, kicked about, and rubbed down, and mistreated . . . and repolished, and knocked around and dusted and sat on or slept in or eaten off of before it develops its real character.

Edna Ferber (1887–1968)
American writer

My two brothers, my sister, and I
would snuggle in Mom's lap while she
read to us. . . . It was in that big, tan
chair where we all used to curl up
together that I learned to love stories
and their magic.

Cyntbia DeFelice (b. 1951)
American writer

A yard like this is more comfortable than most people know. It is not just a yard. It is like an extended living room.

Alice Walker (b. 1944)
American writer

On the front porch of a home . . . these
elders constantly evoke a memory to
bridge past times with the present.

William Ferris (b. 1942)
American writer

Evenings were spent mainly on the back porches where screen doors slammed in the darkness with those really very special summertime sounds.

Lorraine Hansberry (1930–1965)
American playwright

Where the Heart Is

It is the laugh of a baby, the song of a mother, the strength of a father. Warmth of living hearts, light from happy eyes, kindness, loyalty, comradeship. . . . Where joy is shared and sorrow eased. . . . Where even the teakettle sings from happiness. That is home.

Ernestine Schumann-Heink (1861–1936)
Austrian opera singer

Family jokes, though rightly cursed
by strangers, are the bond that keeps
most families alive.

Stella Benson (1892–1933)
English writer

To be happy at home is the ultimate result of all ambition.

Samuel Johnson (1709–1784)
English writer

A good laugh is sunshine in a house.

William Makepeace Thackeray
(1811–1863)
English writer

Home is not where you live but where
they understand you.

Christian Morgenstern (1871–1914)
German poet

Home is the place where, when you have to go there, They have to take you in.

Robert Frost (1874–1963)
American poet

It is very difficult to understand anybody without visiting his home. Houses reveal character.

Gilbert Highet (1906–1978)
American writer

The bedrock of individual success
in life is securing the friendship,
the confidence, the respect of your
next-door neighbor in your little
community in which you live.

Booker T. Washington (1856–1919)
American educator

Not many sounds in life, and I include all urban and all rural sounds, exceed in interest a knock at the door.

Charles Lamb (1775–1834)
English essayist and critic

The ornament of a house is the friends who frequent it.

Ralph Waldo Emerson (1803–1882)
American essayist and poet

A house empty of children and friends is as useless and forlorn as a railroad station on an abandoned line.

Anonymous

Your home can be a place where flowers bloom, children laugh, and music fills the air.

Pam Young
20th-century American homemaker

I love houses that have the flotsam and jetsam of well-lived lives trailing from every surface . . . phone numbers and children's heights written on the walls, and heaps of seashells on the window sills, and skis stuck in the corner and ironing boards open in the kitchen.

Nancy Eberle
20th-century American writer

Unfortunately, the uncontrollable
urge to create has inspired my children
to paint the downstairs, carve boats
out of wooden utensils, construct all
descriptions of machinery and armor
from anything movable in the garage.
Our household could best be described
as a collison between a workshop and
a gymnasium.

Stephen Wonderli (b. 1958)
American writer

It was the policy of the good old gentleman to make his children feel that home was the happiest place in the world; and I value this delicious home-feeling as one of the choicest gifts a parent can bestow.

Washington Irving (1783–1859)
American writer

The happiest moments of my life
have been the few which I have passed
at home in the bosom of my family.

Thomas Jefferson (1743–1826)
Third American president

Without hearts there is no home.

George Gordon, Lord Byron (1788–1824)
English poet

Home is not just a place to sleep,
home is where we house our souls.

Alexandra Stoddard (b. 1941)
American interior designer

A small house well filled is better than an empty palace.

Thomas D. Haliburton (1796–1865)
Canadian jurist and writer

Ah! There is nothing like staying at home for real comfort.

Jane Austen (1775–1817)
English writer

Shut the door. Not that it lets in the
cold but that it lets out the coziness.

> *Mark Twain (1835–1910)*
> *American writer*

There is no place more delightful than one's own fireside.

Marcus Tullius Cicero (106–43 B.C.)
Roman orator, statesman, and philosopher

There is a magic in that little word—it is a mystic circle that surrounds comforts and virtues never known beyond its hallowed limits.

Robert Southey (1774–1843)
English poet

Old houses, I thought, do not belong to people ever, not really, people belong to them.

Gladys Taber (1899–1980)
American archaeologist and writer

One's own surroundings means
so much to one, when one is feeling
miserable.

Edith Sitwell (1887–1964)
English poet, editor, and critic

from "It's a Wonderful House"

Each time I watched It's a Wonderful Life *I was waiting for what I still believe is the most romantic moment in cinema. True love expressed not between two people, but between two people and a house. It is that instant when George Bailey rushes to the abandoned Granville place and realizes that he has, indeed come home. Every inch of space in that old house is a testament to home and faith. Never have there been more beautiful curtains than the checkered cloth tacked over the windows. Never has a fire burned brighter in any fireplace. Walk inside, and you never want to leave. Enter, and everything you wished for just might come true. . . .*

And so I became a convert to Architecture According to Capra. The basic creed is a simple one, easy enough for a child to appreciate and understand: The house of a truly happy family starts out as an abandoned shell. Always. It is a place of cobwebs and ghosts, and the rain doesn't just leak through the holes in the roof, it pours buckets. Forlorn and neglected, hidden behind hedges and a rickety white fence, it is such a disaster not even the people who live right next door appreciate the gorgeous core of this house. They walk on by without a second look. Generations of mice have lived in the pantry. Beams have been destroyed by termites. Windows have been broken by wishing stones thrown from the safety of the sidewalk. Carpenters and plumbers are all very well, but Capra makes one thing perfectly clear: Only love can transform this house. Only love will do.

. . . when George Bailey walks through the door of 320 Sycamore, even at his darkest

hour, anyone can immediately see what it takes an angel to point out to him: Here is a house abundant with life. Busy and hectic and disorganized, but so homey and warm that every object seems illuminated by love, from the newel post that comes off in your

hand to the framed butterflies on the wall to the upright piano that is never in tune.

This sense that you are really, truly home cannot be drawn up like a blueprint. It never depends on how many hollyhocks are planted beside the garden gate. It doesn't even matter if the front door leads to a three-bedroom ranch exactly like every other on the block or a Victorian high up on a hill.... It's any house where the children sleep peacefully in their beds on winter nights, dreaming beneath warm quilts. It's any address where you realize—perhaps at long last—your own good fortune.

Alice Hoffman (b. 1952)
American writer

The ache for home lives in all of us, the safe place where we can go as we are and not be questioned.

Maya Angelou (b. 1928)
American writer

To paraphrase Robert Frost, home
is the place where they have to let
you walk around in your socks,
because in all likelihood they are
shoeless themselves.

Laura Green
20th-century American journalist

A happy home . . . the single spot of rest which a man has upon this earth for the cultivation of his noblest sensibilities.

Harvey Green (b. 1946)
American historian

Almost any man worthy of his salt
would fight to defend his home, but no
one ever heard of a man going to war
for his boarding house.

Mark Twain (1835–1910)
American writer

A home is no home unless it contains food and fire for the mind as well as for the body.

Sarah Margaret Fuller (1810–1850)
American critic and social reformer

In happy homes he saw the light
Of household fires gleam warm
    and bright.

Henry Wadsworth Longfellow (1807–1882)
American poet

When the lamps in the house are
lighted it is like the flowering of lotus
on the lake.

Chinese proverb

The first indication of domestic
happiness is the love of one's home.

Francis D. Montlosier (1755–1838)
French publicist

Whatever brawls disturb the street,
There should be peace at home.

Isaac Watts (1674–1748)
English cleric

A home is not a mere transient shelter: its essence lies in its permanence, in its capacity for accretion and solidification, in its quality of representing, in all its details, the personalities of the people who live in it.

H. L. Mencken (1880–1956)
American writer

Home is where Affection calls,
Filled with shrines the heart
hath builded.

Charles Swain (1801–1874)
English writer

When love adorns a home,
other ornaments are secondary.

Anonymous

To Adam, Paradise was home.
To the good among his descendants
home is paradise.

Julius Charles Hare (1795–1855)
English translator

Homeward Bound

If we return to the old home as to a
nest, it is because memories are dreams,
because the home of other days has
become a great image of lost intimacy.

Gaston Bachelard (1884–1962)
French philosopher and writer

You can't appreciate home till you've left it. . . .

O. Henry [William Sydney Porter]
(1862–1910)
American writer

But the roots remain. The roots that will forever keep calling you back, begging, "Come home."

Marjorie Holmes (b. 1910)
American writer

I know not why, but home is dearest.

Marcus Tullius Cicero (106–43 B.C.)
Roman orator, statesman, and philosopher

from "Roofs"

If you call a gypsy a vagabond, I think
  you do him wrong,
For he never goes a-traveling but he
  takes his home along.
And the only reason a road is good, as
  every wanderer knows,
Is just because of the homes, the homes,
  the homes to which it goes.

They say that life is a highway and its
milestones are the years,
And now and then there's a toll-gate
where you buy your way with tears.
It's a rough road and a steep road and
it stretches broad and far,
But it leads at last to a golden Town
where golden Houses are.

Joyce Kilmer (1886–1918)
American poet

To know after absence the familiar
street and road and village and house is
to know again the satisfaction of home.

Harold Borland (1900–1978)
American writer

Only that traveling is good which reveals to me the value of home and enables me to enjoy it better.

Henry David Thoreau (1817–1862)
American writer and naturalist

'Tis sweet to hear the watch-dog's honest bark

Bay deep-mouth'd welcome as we draw

near home;

'Tis sweet to know there is an eye will mark

Our coming, and look brighter when

we come.

George Gordon, Lord Byron (1788–1824)
English poet

I cannot tell you . . . how much I enjoy
home after having been deprived of one
for so long, for our dwelling in New
York and Philadelphia was not home,
only a sojourning. The General and
I feel like children just released from
school or from a hard taskmaster. . . .
We are so penurious with our
enjoyment that we are loath to share
it with anyone but dear friends. . . .

Martha Washington (1731–1802)
American First Lady

When I was at home, I was in a better place.

William Shakespeare (1564–1616)
English playwright and poet

Our house was not unsentient matter—it had a heart and a soul, and eyes to see with; and approvals and solicitudes and deep sympathies; it was us, and we were in its confidence and lived in its grace and in the peace of its benedictions. We never came home from an absence that its face did not light up and speak out in eloquent welcome—and we could not enter it unmoved.

Mark Twain (1835–1910)
American writer

Where we love is home. Home that our feet may leave but not our hearts.

Oliver Wendell Holmes Jr. (1841–1935)
American jurist

You leave home to seek your fortune
and when you get it you go home
and share it with your family.

Anita Baker (b. 1958)
American singer

A man travels the world in search
of what he needs and returns home
to find it.

George Moore (1852–1933)
English writer

Whether you're a woman or a man, when you're out there fighting the world, you want to come home and find peace.

John H. Clarke (1857–1945)
American jurist

What did Vlysses wish in the middest of his trauailing, but onely to see the smoake of his owne Chymnie.

John Lyly (1554–1606)
English writer

Home is the place
where life makes up its mind.

Anonymous